Animal Superstars

SUPERSTAR INSECTS

Louise Spilsbury

Raintree is an imprint of Capstone Global Library Limited, a company incorporated in England and Wales having its registered office at 264 Banbury Road, Oxford, OX2 7DY - Registered company number: 6695582

www.raintree.co.uk
myorders@raintree.co.uk

Produced for Raintree by Calcium
Editor for Calcium: Sarah Eason
Designer for Calcium: Paul Myerscough
Designer for Raintree: Cynthia Della Rovere
Production by Katy LaVigne
Printed and bound in India

ISBN 978 1 4747 6523 7 (hardback)
22 21 20 19 18
10 9 8 7 6 5 4 3 2 1

ISBN 978 1 4747 6527 5 (paperback)
23 22 21 20 19
10 9 8 7 6 5 4 3 2 1

British Library Cataloguing in Publication Data
A full catalogue record for this book is available from the British Library.

Acknowledgements
We would like to thank the following for permission to reproduce photographs:
Cover: Shutterstock: Gnatuk (left), MongPro (top), Daniel Prudek (right). Inside: Dreamstime: Rinus Baak 29b, Claudiodivizia 23t, Martine De Graaf 17, Isselee 2–3, 26, 27, Johan Larson 21t, Liumangtiger 19t, Paul Looyen 24, Mirage1 20, Orionmystery 21b, Marc Parsons 28, Kantilal Patel 23b, Skynetphoto 19b; Shutterstock: Alle 29t, Andrey Gorshkov 5t, Charles Harker 14bg, Matt Jeppson 13, Yuriy Kulik 18, Lightbox 8, Lkordela 11b, Dr. Morley Read 7t, Rtbilder 10, 11t, Sandiren 15t, Sarah2 7b, Joseph Scott Photography 25, South12th Photography 16, Takepicsforfun 4, Tompi 5b, Marco Uliana 1, 12, Dennis van de Water 6, Wonderisland 9t, 9b, Worldswildlifewonders 22; Wikimedia Commons: P.E. Bragg 14, Dr. Aaron T. Dossey 15b.

Contents

Insects

There are about one million different types of insect across the world. Some are smaller than a full stop, while others have wings that measure 27 centimetres across. Some can survive in the hottest deserts and others in the freezing cold of Antarctica. Despite their differences, all insects have some things in common.

All insects lay eggs that hatch into young. Some resemble adults, others look completely different.

All insects have six legs.

All insects are **invertebrates**. They have a tough outer layer called an exoskeleton, which protects their body.

Most insects have wings.

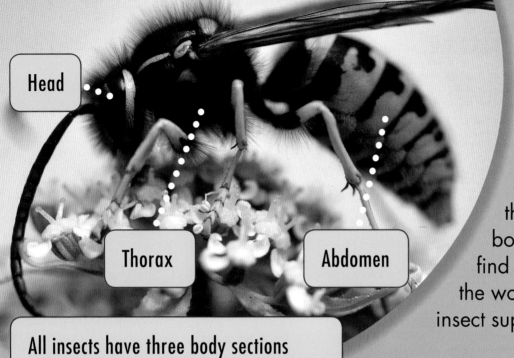

Head

Thorax

Abdomen

All insects have three body sections called the head, **thorax** and **abdomen**.

Insect superstars

All insects are amazing, but some are more astonishing than others! In this book we are going to find out about some of the world's most talented insect superstars.

Secret stars

The hawk moth goes to great lengths to reach its food. It feeds on a sugary juice called nectar found deep inside particular types of orchid. To reach its target the moth has a tube-shaped tongue that is 27 cm long. The tongue coils up neatly inside the moth's mouth when it is not in use.

Froghopper

This small insect's name indicates that it can jump like a frog! The froghopper is only half a centimetre long but can leap 71 centimetres into the air from standing. That is the equivalent of an adult human jumping over a skyscraper!

After its take-off jump, the froghopper may also use its wings to fly further away.

The froghopper's mouth is shaped like a straw. The insect pokes its straw-like mouth into plants it hops onto and drinks the liquid inside.

6

Quick getaway

The froghopper does not jump high for glory, but for survival. When a froghopper spots an approaching hungry bird or another **predator**, it quickly hops away. The froghopper nymph is called the spittlebug. It is so called because it covers itself in a bubbly blanket of spit, beneath which the insect hides from predators.

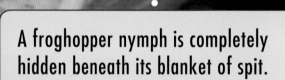

A froghopper nymph is completely hidden beneath its blanket of spit.

Secret stars

Cat fleas are also great jumpers. They jump by pressing and releasing rubbery pads inside their knees. Cat fleas hop to escape the scratching claws of a host cat, or its tongue when it grooms itself. They also hop to land on a new cat on which to live and feed.

Rhinoceros beetle

Gram for gram, rhinoceros beetles are the world's strongest creatures. They can lift 850 times their own weight. That is the equivalent of a human lifting 10 adult elephants! Rhinoceros beetles use their great strength to burrow through soil and push aside wood and other debris found on the forest floor.

The male rhinoceros beetle has one or two horns on its thorax and one on the top of its head.

The thick, tough exoskeleton of the rhinoceros beetle protects it from some predators.

8

Top talent

Rhinoceros beetles have the heaviest babies of all insects. Their **larvae** can weigh nearly 225g. They grow so large by spending all day eating rotting wood on the forest floor. Adults eat only fruit and tree sap.

Battle to mate

Male beetles fight over a female beetle that is ready to mate. The males use their horns to push over their opponents. They even pick up their rivals in their horns and then slam them onto the ground. Females mate with the winner because that male has proven its fitness and may help the female produce healthy young beetles.

Male beetles fight to show their strength to females.

9

Honeybee

Honeybees can do some great dance moves! The bees live together in a large group in a hive. Some members of the group have the job of finding flowers to feed on. If successful, the bees return to the hive and perform a special wiggle dance. The dance shows other bees where to find the flowers so they can help fetch food for the hive.

As part of its wiggle dance, a bee shakes its abdomen from side to side while walking in one direction.

The honeybee's wiggle dance shows other bees how close food is and in which direction to fly to find it.

Young bees develop in honeycomb holes. There, they eat food and grow quickly.

10

Honey stores

Worker bees collect nectar from flowers in the summer to make honey. This sweet food is stored in the honeycomb for the bees to eat in winter, when there are no flowers to feed on. The wiggle dance shows worker bees where to find food quickly so they can fill the honey stores in preparation for the winter ahead.

When honeybees work together to collect lots of food, hives often hold spare honey that people can eat.

Top talent

As they feed, honeybees carry tiny grains called **pollen** from one flower to another. This is called **pollination** and helps plants make fruit and seeds. Just one honeybee visits between 50 and 1,000 flowers on every trip from the hive. Imagine how many plants are pollinated by a **colony**!

11

Silk moth

Imagine being able to smell something from nearly 10 kilometres away. The male silk moth can do just that! This superstar sniffer smells using giant feathery structures called **antennae**. The male uses the antennae to sniff a special perfume, called a pheromone, which is produced by female silk moths.

> The antennae above the moth's eyes are covered in hairs. The entire surface of each hair is covered with smell detectors.

The right smell

Adult silk moths live for only a few weeks. Their most important task in that time is to produce young. Different types of female moth produce different pheromones. Only the male silk moth can detect the pheromone of the female silk moth. His smell detectors are like locks and the pheromones are like keys that fit them.

The moth's wings and body are covered with furry scales to help it keep warm when it is active at night.

Top talent

The greediest insects are probably caterpillars, which are the young of butterflies and moths. A silk moth caterpillar eats 86,000 times its own body weight of leaves in the first two months of its life. That is the equivalent of a kitten eating more than 12.7 tonnes of food!

Chan's megastick

Stick insects are long-bodied creatures that usually look like brown-grey twigs. Chan's megastick is one of the longest of all. Its body is an amazing 35.5 centimetres long. With its front legs extended, the insect reaches 56 centimetres long, which is the length of a human arm!

This stick insect's body is long and smooth, but other types have flaps on their legs and abdomens that look like dried leaves.

The female Chan's megastick is two-thirds bigger than the male.

The insect has a small head with small antennae. The head is hidden when the front legs are extended.

Master of disguise

Stick insects resemble twigs to **camouflage** themselves from predators, including birds. Even the eggs of Chan's megastick are camouflaged. They look like brown seeds with tiny wings, and float down to the ground as the female lays them.

Stick insects usually remain still for long periods, but sometimes sway to mimic branches moving in the wind.

Secret stars

If a predator gets too close, some stick insects flash colourful wings to startle it. The devil rider is a small, stripy stick insect that can squirt milky poison from its thorax at a predator more than 38 centimetres away.

15

Tarantula hawk wasp

At about 5.5 centimetres long, the terrifying tarantula hawk wasp is the largest wasp in the world. Females have enormous stingers measuring up to 0.8 cm long. These weapons deliver a very painful sting. The tarantula hawk wasp uses its sting mainly to attack tarantula spiders.

The wasp has large eyes to look for spiders or the burrows that they make.

The stinger injects a large amount of **venom** into its victim.

The wasp's legs have hooks that grasp tarantulas.

The tarantula hawk wasp strikes the spider's soft abdomen when it lifts up its front legs.

Spider slayer

The female tarantula hawk wasp hunts tarantulas. She taps the spider's web to entice it out, then quickly stings it. The female's venom paralyses the spider in seconds. Then, the female drags the spider into a burrow, lays an egg on it and seals the burrow. The young larva that hatches from the egg then eats the spider while it is still alive!

Secret stars

The prize for smallest insect in the world goes to the fairyfly wasp. The tarantula hawk wasp is 450 times longer than this tiny insect. Fairyfly wasps hunt for butterfly eggs on which to lay their own eggs. The larvae that hatch from the eggs then feed on the butterfly eggs.

Cicada

Never stand too close to a male cicada when it is singing to attract a female. This crooner's rasping sound measures up to 120 decibels. That is as loud as a jet engine! The cicada is not affected by its chirping because it muffles its own hearing when it calls so it is not deafened.

The cicada's eyes are positioned wide apart on its head to allow it to see all around for predators such as birds.

The cicada looks a bit like a locust but is actually a relative of the froghopper.

Parts of the cicada's abdomen shrink and then extend to make its sound, rather like the way a person can crush and uncrush an empty plastic bottle.

18

Sing to survive

Male cicadas fly to trees near females. There, they begin to sing. The female flicks her wings if she is impressed by the male's song and wants to mate. She lays eggs inside a twig and young, called nymphs, hatch. The nymphs burrow underground. They may remain there, feeding on root juices, for 17 years before turning into adults.

The skin of the wingless cicada nymph splits open to reveal a winged adult inside!

Secret stars

The mole cricket uses a trick to make its call even louder than that of a male cicada. It makes a cone-shaped entrance to its underground burrow that has the effect of a megaphone. A person can hear a mole cricket calling from its burrow from 610 metres away!

19

Praying mantis

The praying mantis is the only insect that can turn its head a full 180 degrees! That is what makes the insect such an expert predator. The mantis twists its triangular head to look all around for insects and even frogs to eat. Female mantises have a strange food craving, they are rather partial to eating the males after mating!

The mantis's green colour camouflages the insect in the trees in which it lives.

Part of the mantis's thorax forms a neck so the insect can stretch its head forward to look at its **prey**.

Long outer wing covers hide bright red wings beneath that frighten off predators.

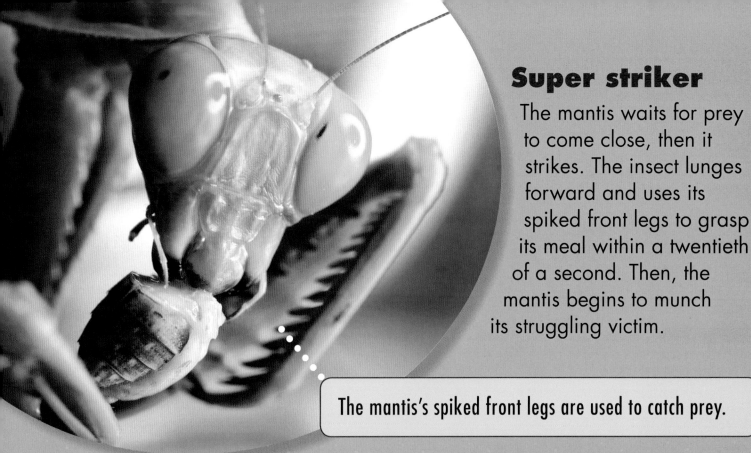

Super striker

The mantis waits for prey to come close, then it strikes. The insect lunges forward and uses its spiked front legs to grasp its meal within a twentieth of a second. Then, the mantis begins to munch its struggling victim.

The mantis's spiked front legs are used to catch prey.

Secret stars

The fastest strike of any insect predator is made by the trap-jaw ant. It closes its jaws more than 2,000 times faster than a person can blink. The jaws move so quickly and clamp together so hard that the ant jumps into the air with the force!

Dragonfly

What insect is as fast as a leopard? The Australian dragonfly! This is the world's fastest-flying insect, reaching an incredible 58 kilometres per hour. The dragonfly flies so quickly to chase flying insects, such as mosquitoes, to eat. Not only does the insect chase its victim at speed, it also works out its prey's speed and direction so it can intercept it in mid-air.

The dragonfly's long abdomen helps it balance while moving through the air.

The dragonfly's deep thorax is packed with muscles that move its wings up and down and side to side.

The dragonfly has two sets of large, transparent wings.

Secret stars

The largest dragonfly today has wings that measure 19 centimetres across. That is tiny compared to the dragonflies of 300 million years ago, which had wingspans four times greater. We know these giant insects existed from the **fossil** remains people have found.

Acrobatic performer

Not only does a dragonfly fly forwards, this accomplished acrobat can change direction in mid-air and fly sideways or backwards. It can also hover on the spot. That is because its wings can beat and twist independently of each other, rather like the blades of a helicopter.

Dragonflies are masters of the air. Of all insects, they are the most acrobatic flyers.

Bull ant

Bull ants live in colonies and the worker ants defend the group, by attack! These 5-centimetre ants are the most dangerous in the world. If something approaches their nest, the ants attack it. They are also called bulldog ants because once they bite, they do not let go and continuously sting their victim with venom.

The ant's large eyes can see approaching danger from up to 1 metre away.

The venom in the stinger at the end of the ant's abdomen is one of the most painful of all insects.

The ant's jaws look a bit like a toothed beak. Powerful muscles clamp them tightly together.

Lethal attack

Bull ant venom increases the human heart rate and can cause fever and an **allergic reaction**. For some people, a bull ant attack can be deadly. Bull ants also sting insects they take back to the nest to feed to larvae. The aggressive action of the bull ant helps ensure its survival and makes it a successful species.

A lone bull ant is a formidable hunter, but an entire group of these creatures is a powerful killing force.

Top talent

Some bull ants have an additional method of attack. Jack jumper ants can leap eight times the length of their body when attacking intruders near the nest. Jack jumper ants collect nectar and juices from bugs to feed to their larvae.

Water boatman

Water boatmen are insect superstars that travel across ponds by rowing. However, unlike rowers at the Olympics, these creatures travel upside-down! The water boatman lies on its back on the water's surface and uses its long back legs to push itself across.

The insect's back legs have a wide, flat shape a little like a paddle. The legs push aside water and move the insect forward.

Short front legs are used to grab prey.

The water boatmen's body is streamlined to help it move through the water easily, like a rowing boat.

26

Speedy hunters

Water boatmen row to hunt for prey. The insects spend much of their time resting on the water's surface, waiting to sense the movements of prey. When they feel any vibrations below, the water boatmen row quickly across the water to find their meal.

Top talent

Water boatmen cannot breathe underwater so, just like scuba divers, they carry an air supply. They cling to a bubble of air, which also acts as a buoyancy vest to stop the creature sinking when it dives in pursuit of underwater animals.

Amazing adaptations

Some insects are superstars because they have developed body features to help them survive. This is called physical **adaptation.** For example, the tarantula hawk wasp has developed a powerful venom to help it kill tarantulas and the silk moth has developed antennae that help it locate a mate.

Some moths have patterns and colours that look like tree bark to camouflage them. This protects the moths from hungry birds.

Behavioural adaptations

Some adaptations are behavioural. These are things that animals do to survive. For example, stick insects remain still so their long bodies more closely resemble twigs, and bull ants attack intruders to defend their colony.

Some caddis fly larvae make a case of pieces of gravel in which to hide as they grow.

Many insects become adults together to increase their chances of finding a mate and to lessen the likelihood of being eaten by predators.

Top talent

One insect top talent is the ability to develop from egg to adult quickly. Many types of insects lay numerous eggs. They do so because most will be eaten or destroyed after they hatch, preventing them from growing into adults that can produce eggs themselves.

Glossary

abdomen central section of an insect

adaptation feature or way of behaving that helps an animal survive

allergic reaction situation in which the body reacts badly to a particular food or substance

antennae pair of sense organs located on the front of an insect's head

camouflage natural colouring or shape of an animal that allows it to blend in with its surroundings

colony group of insects that live and work together

fossil remains of an ancient animal

invertebrates animals without a backbone

larvae wingless form of insects when they first hatch

pollen fine powder produced by plants

pollination transfer of pollen from one flower to another so the second flower can produce seeds that grow into new plants

predator animal that hunts and eats other animals

prey animal that is hunted and eaten by other animals

thorax part of an insect's body between its head and abdomen

venom poison

Further reading

British Insects: A Photographic Guide (Nature Detectives), Victoria Munson (Wayland, 2016)

Insect Emporium, Susie Brooks (Red Shed, 2016)

Insect: Explore the world of insects and creepy-crawlies (Eyewitness), Various authors (DK Children, 2017)

Minibeasts (The Great Nature Hunt) Cath Senker, (Franklin Watts, 2016)

Websites

www.dkfindout.com/uk/animals-and-nature/insects/
Find out more about some of your favourite insects!

www.nationalgeographic.com/animals/invertebrates/
Read stories and watch videos to learn more about why insects are such successful animals.

Index